CHARMS
OF HARMS

THE CHARMS OF HARMS

Selected Poems by Daniil Kharms
as Translated by Svetlana Dubovitskaya
and Illustrated by Ksenia Kolosova

Matteo Publishing

2011

Published in the United Kingdom by:
Matteo Publishing
16 Sutton Court Road,
London, W4 4NG, UK
email: matteopublishing@gmail.com

Kharms, Daniil.

The Charms of Harms
Selected poems by Daniil Kharms
[Translated from the original Russian]

First printed in October 2011

Project managed and produced by Svetlana Dubovitskaya.
Illustrations by Ksenia Kolosova.
Layout and design by Katerina Akhtyrskaya.

ISBN 978 0 9570649 1 1

Hello!

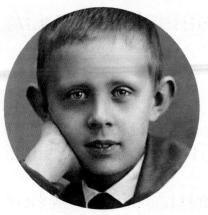

Contents

07 ▶

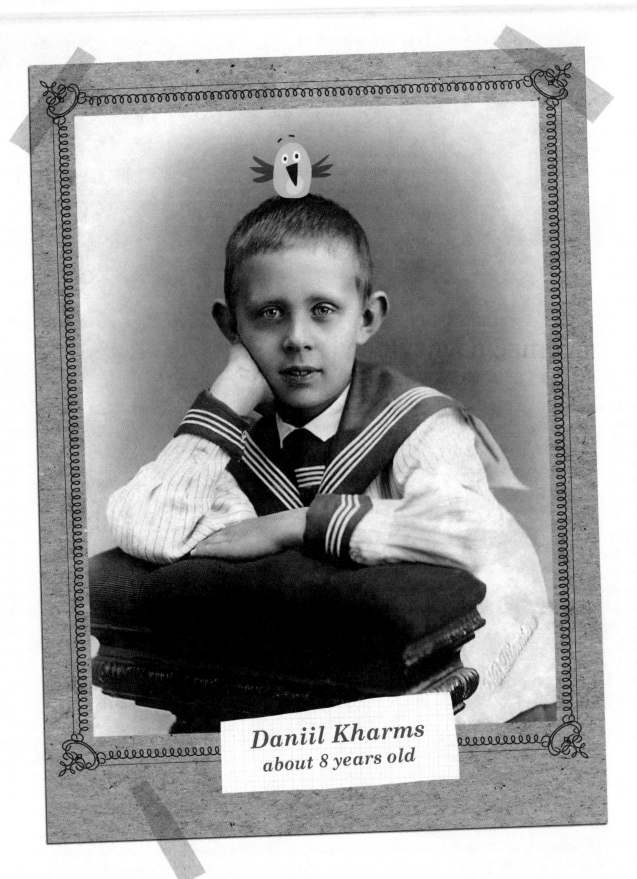

Daniil Kharms
about 8 years old

Foreword

Dear reader!

You are holding in your hands a book by a great Russian poet, a strange, interesting, hugely unusual and eccentric man by the name of Daniil Kharms. He was born in 1905 in St. Petersburg when Russia was still the empire ruled by the tsar. Then, in 1917 Russia was forever transformed by the revolution, the tsar was deposed and the country became known as the Soviet Union. St Petersburg started being called Leningrad.

Everything changed, many things became better for the working people of Russia, they received free education and medical care, all of them were taught how to read and write. At the same time many other things, little by little, became worse. For example, being unusual and not like everybody else became a crime. So the times for poets and various other artists as well as all creative people in general became very dire.

So, Daniil Kharms grew up and became a poet and a writer in the country which, in those days, did not welcome individuality and did not strive to nourish its poets. The choice was simple: a person was either willing to become like everybody else or was forcibly removed from society, taken to gaol or even killed.

Daniil Kharms was first arrested, and afterwards forced off the major magazines of the day into the children's literature. It was supposed to be his punishment but he created beautiful verses for children and they loved him in return. However, since he did not stop writing and being funny, Kharms was eventually arrested again and kept in prison where he died in 1942. Even to mention his name was a crime – until the 1990s when Russia changed yet again and recognised the wrong that she did to her poets. And this is why it is possible for you to hold this book in your hands today. Daniil Kharms deserved his right to be known and loved by you.

The book was translated from its original Russian by Svetlana Dubovitskaya. The brilliant illustrations were performed by a talented Russian artist Ksenia Kolosova. Some of the pictures show Leningrad in the days when the tall ungainly figure of Daniil Kharms, an ever-present pipe in his mouth, was roaming the city streets and reciting his wonderful enchanting poems to children.

Svetlana Dubovitskaya

THE JACKDAW.

For Ian and Dasha

Didn't I Run...

Didn't I run and didn't I scamper
To and fro!
I got tired, so I sat
And ran no more.

What's that flying in the sky?
A jackdaw.
And what's flying after him?
A jackdaw.
And another one again?
A jackdaw.
And one more that's after him?
A jackdaw.
So how come I do not fly?
What a bore!

I got tired of sitting round,
I would like to fly around,
Take a run,
Spread my wings,
Be a bird and fly around.

11 ▶

I ran out, jumping, skipping,
Cried hey-ho,
My heals were clicking,
And my arms went flailing round,
I was hopping up and down.

Lo, a hawk is guarding me,
And the wind is pushing me,
Woods and rivers flashing by,
And above me – the blue sky.

I got tired of being a hawk,
Felt like going for a walk.
Pitter-
Patter,
Pitter-
Patter,
I am going for a walk.

13 ▶

In a garden I am walking,
All the flowers I am picking,
Up an apple tree I'm climbing
And the apples I am hurling.
I was throwing apples deftly:
Hit or miss I apples threw,
And I hit the sky directly,
And I pierced the cloud through.

I felt tired of throwing things,
Felt like swimming in a stream.
Plop-
Plop-
Plop!
I felt like diving in a stream.

15▶

Look, I'm swimming
Underwater,
Close to the river bed,
Look how quick my legs are flipping,
How I steer with my head!

And the folk, from ashore, go:
"Fishes only live in water,
But it is completely true
That the fishes,
Even fishes! –
Do not swim as well as you!"

And I go:
"I'm now fed up with water,
I am moving to dry land.
It's more fun to go tumbling
Go sprawling on the sand!"

17 ▶

I got tired of all this swimming,
So I made it for the shore,
Left and right, and helter-skelter
Started running to and fro.

Didn't I run and didn't I scamper
To and fro!
I got tired, so I sat
And ran no more.

And so on...

17 May 1929

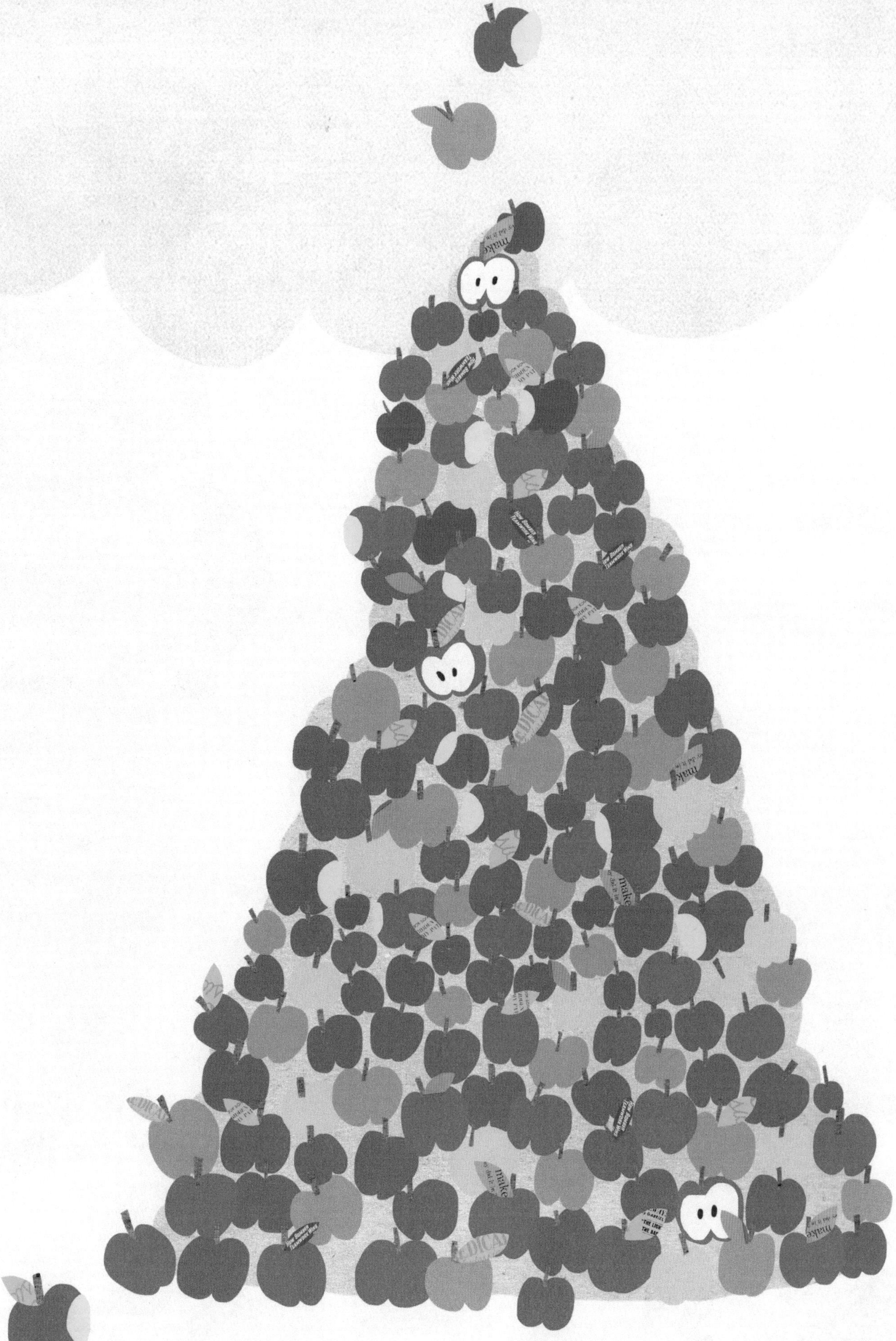

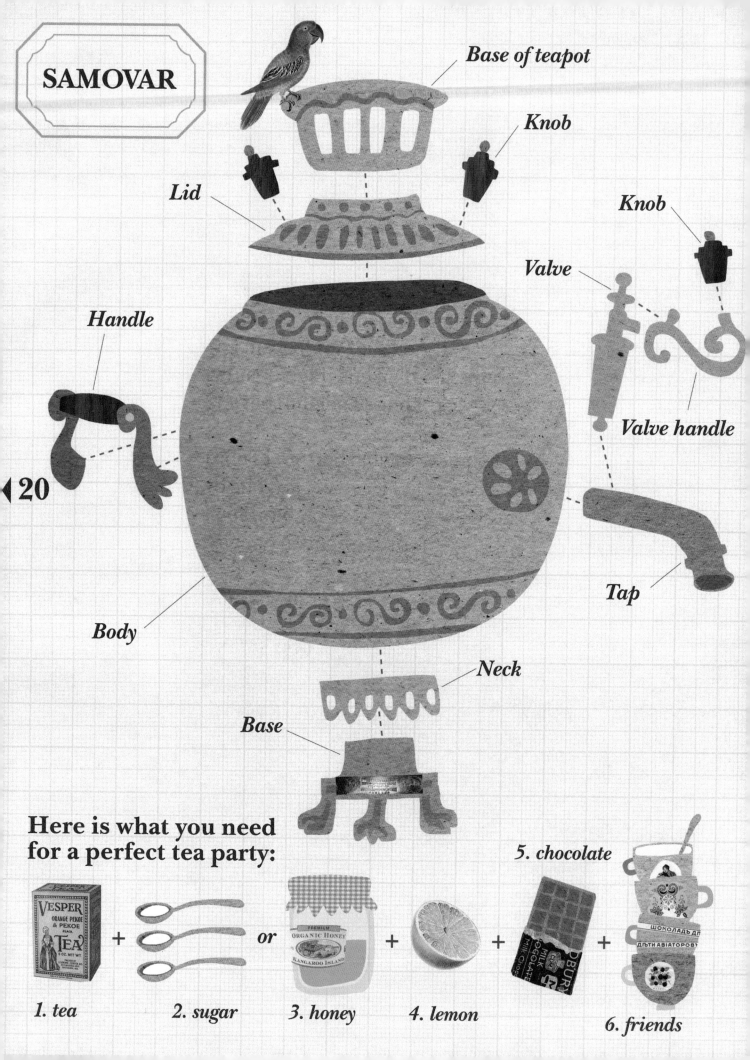

SAMOVAR

Base of teapot

Knob

Lid

Knob

Valve

Handle

Valve handle

20

Tap

Body

Neck

Base

Here is what you need for a perfect tea party:

5. chocolate

1. tea + 2. sugar or 3. honey + 4. lemon + 5. chocolate + 6. friends

VESPER
ORANGE PEKOE
& PEKOE
TEA

ORGANIC HONEY
KANGAROO ISLAND

ШОКОЛАДЪ ДЛ
ДЂТИ АВІАТОРОВЪ

Ivan Ivanych Samovar*

Ivan Ivanych Samovar,
A big-bellied samovar,
Was a jumbo samovar

Where the water boiled within,
Steamy water puffed within,
Boiling water raged within

Running out from the tap,
Through a hole in the tap
In a cup – right from the tap.

* Samovar is a heated metal container
traditionally used to heat and boil water
in and around Russia.

In the morning came to it,
Very early came to it,
Uncle Petya came to it.

He came up to it and said,
"Now I would love," he said,
"To have my morning tea," he said.

Yet another person came,
Glass in hand, she also came,
Auntie Katia also came.

Auntie Katia now said,
"I would also love," she said,
"I would love some tea," she said.

After which the Grandpa came,
He was fragile but he came,
Grandpa in his slippers came.

Gave a yawn and then he said,
"Should I probably," he said,
"Should I have some tea?" he said.

Grandpa

Fido

Granny

That was when the Granny came,
Ancient Granny also came,
Walking stick in hand, she came.

Deep in thought, she now said,
"Would be nice," she now said
"If I had some tea," she said.

And a little girl, she hopped,
To the samovar she hopped,
The granddaughter gaily hopped.

«Pour me now," the small girl said.
"A cup of tea," the small girl said,
"Lots of sugar, please," she said.

Now Fido bounded in,
And the cat came bounding in,
To the samovar came in,

So that they could get some milk,
Some boiled water with some milk,
Nice and tasty, this boiled milk.

Auntie Katya

Uncle Petya

Granddaughter

Cat

After which Seryozha came,
Sleepy and unwashed he came,
After all the others came.

"Serve me tea," he loudly said,
"A cup of tea I want," he said,
"And the biggest one," he said.

They were tilting, they were tipping
Samovar's huge frame
But only steam came puffing out,
Only steam now came.

They were twisting it around
On the table top
But the only thing that came of it
Was drip-drop-drop.

Our dear Samovar,
Our table Samovar,
Golden-hearted Samovar

Boiling water won't serve!
Never will late-comers serve!
Lazy-boots he just won't serve!
So there!

1928

AMAZING TABBY

She damaged her foot, the unfortunate tabby,

And now she's sitting around all day.
Hurry up, there's a cure for this miserable tabby:

A bunch of balloons is the surest way!

And suddenly folk are crowding the high street,
They are nudging each other, they chatter and stare,

While the tabby is partly afoot in the high street
And partly she's suavely afloat in the air!

1938

27 ▶

3

LIAR

– Do you know?
Do you know?
Do you know?
Do you know?
But of course you realise,
Clearly you know!
– No! No! No! No!
We know nothing of the kind,
Haven't heard, and haven't seen it,
Know nothing of the kind!

– Do you realise that MY
Do you realise that DAD –
Do you realise that – DY
THAT MY DADDY – he had children,
Forty tall and handsome sons?
Wasn't twenty, wasn't thirty:
Was exactly forty sons?

– There, there, there, there!
What a lie! Lie! Lie!
Even twenty, even thirty –
Stands a chance and could be fine.
But to say that he had forty –
This is spinning quite a line!

3) 4) 5) 6) 7)

10) 11) 12) 13) 14)

17) 18) 19) 20) 21)

24) 25) 26) 27) 28)

31) 32) 33) 34) 35)

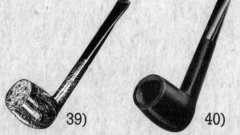

39) 40)

Daniil Kharms loved smoking his pipe and had a huge collection of pipes of all kinds!

— Do you realise that THEM
Do you realise that DOG —
Do you realise that — GIES
THEM THE EVER-BARKING DOGGIES
Now know how to fly?
Just like birds they now can fly?
Not like beasts, and not like fishes —
Just like falcons they can fly?

— There, there, there, there!
What a lie! Lie! Lie!
Even beasts or even fishes —
Stand a chance and could be fine,
But to say they are like falcons —
This is spinning quite a line!

T e s s i n   Basodino
Val Leventina
Bellinzona-   Val Bedretto   P. Rotondo
Lago Ritom ←—Lugano   P. Lucendro
        Airolo   ST GOTTHARD · PASS
                    2108 m

– Do you realise that IN
Do you realise that THE
Do you realise that SKY
IN THE SKY the sun shall vanish,

There will be a wheel instead!
It will be completely golden,
Not a plate and not a patty –
A tremendous wheel instead!

– There, there, there, there!
What a lie! Lie! Lie!
Say, a plate, or even patty –
Stands a chance and could be fine.

But a wheel completely golden –
This is spinning quite a line!

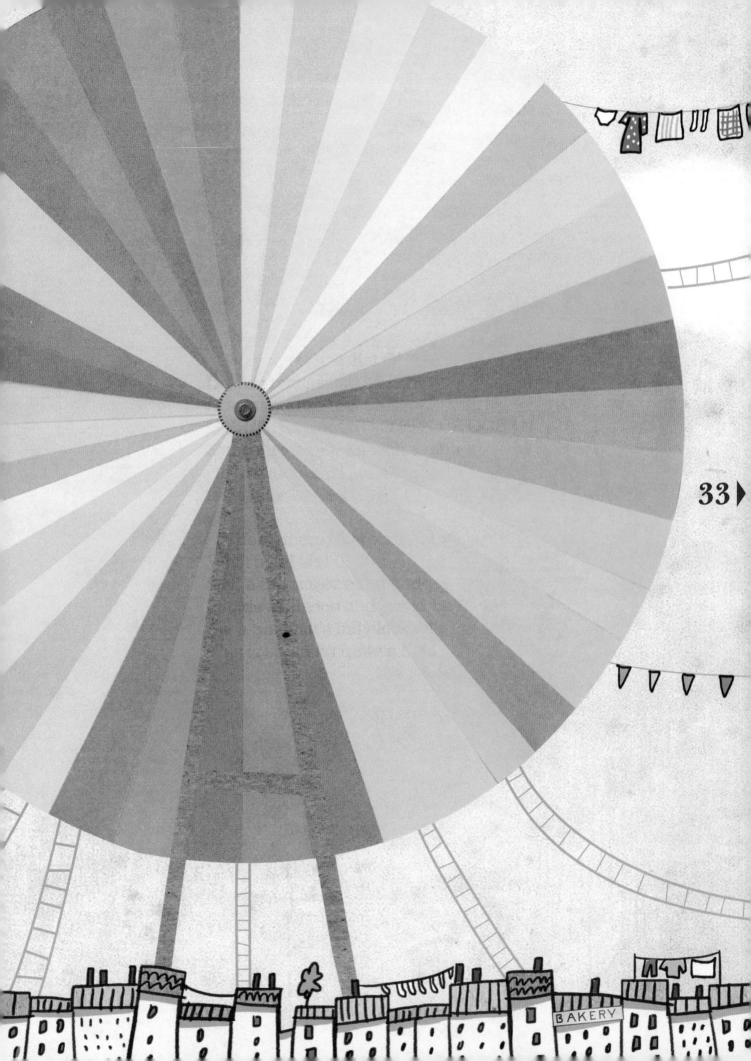

33 ▶

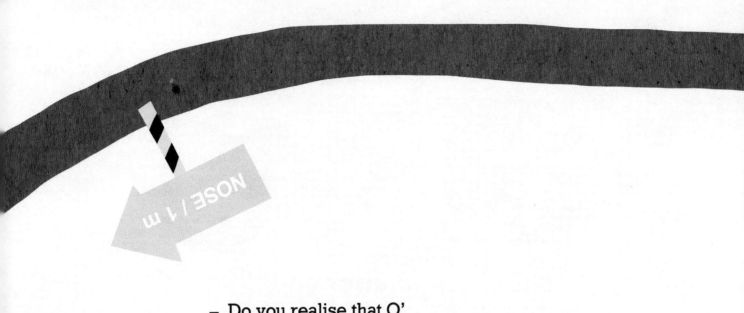

– Do you realise that O'
Do you realise that –VER
Do you realise that SEA
O'ER THE SEA AND O'ER THE OCEAN
Stands a watchman with a gun!
Not a broom and not a cudgel –
It's a fully loaded gun!

– There, there, there, there!
What a lie! Lie! Lie!
Say, a broom, or even cudgel –
Stands a chance and could be fine.
But a gun that's fully loaded –
This is spinning quite a line!

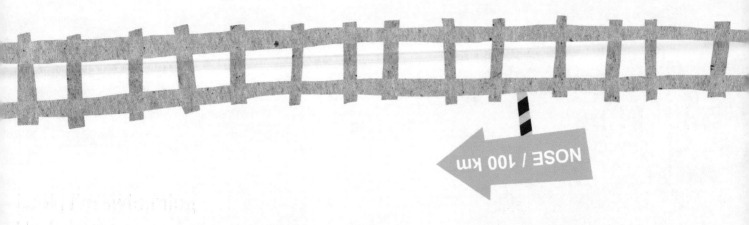

NOSE / 100 km

– Do you realise that TO
Do you realise that YOUR
Do you realise that NOSE
TO YOUR NOSE there's such a distance

Can't be covered, not at all!
Can't be reached by hands nor toes,
Can't be touched by no fingers,
Can be neither reached nor touched!

36

– There, there, there, there!
What a lie! Lie! Lie!
Well, to ride, or run, or go –
Stands a chance, and could be fine
But to reach your nose with fingers –
This is spinning quite a line!

1930

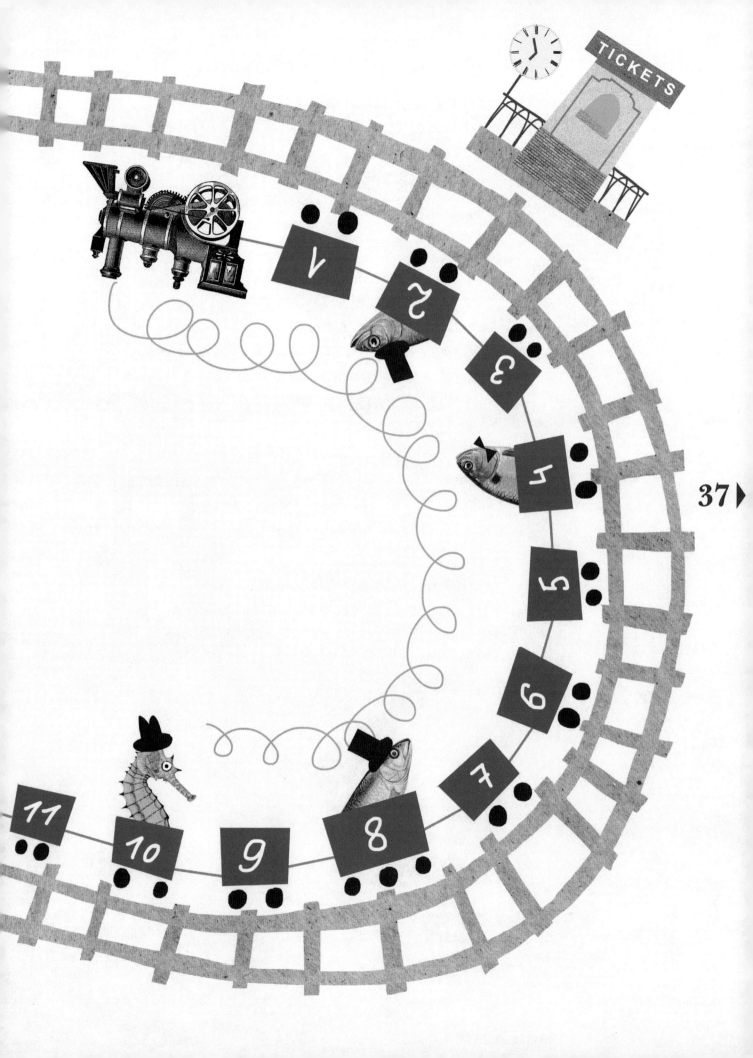

IVAN TOPORYSHKIN

4. log

Young Ivan went hunting, rifles ready to fire,
The hound gave chase over the fence with a swish.
Our Ivan, like a log, tumbled in a quagmire
And the hound in a river is feeding the fish.

9. fish

Our Ivan went hunting, rifles ready to fire,
The hound gave chase bounding forth like a fish.
Our Ivan, like a log, fell across the quagmire
And the hound, in the river, jumped the fence with a swish.

Our Ivan went hunting, rifles ready to fire,
The hound, in the river, fell down with a swish.
Young Ivan, like a log, leapt across the quagmire
And the hound jumped forward and fell on a fish.

1928

2. dog

38

6. river

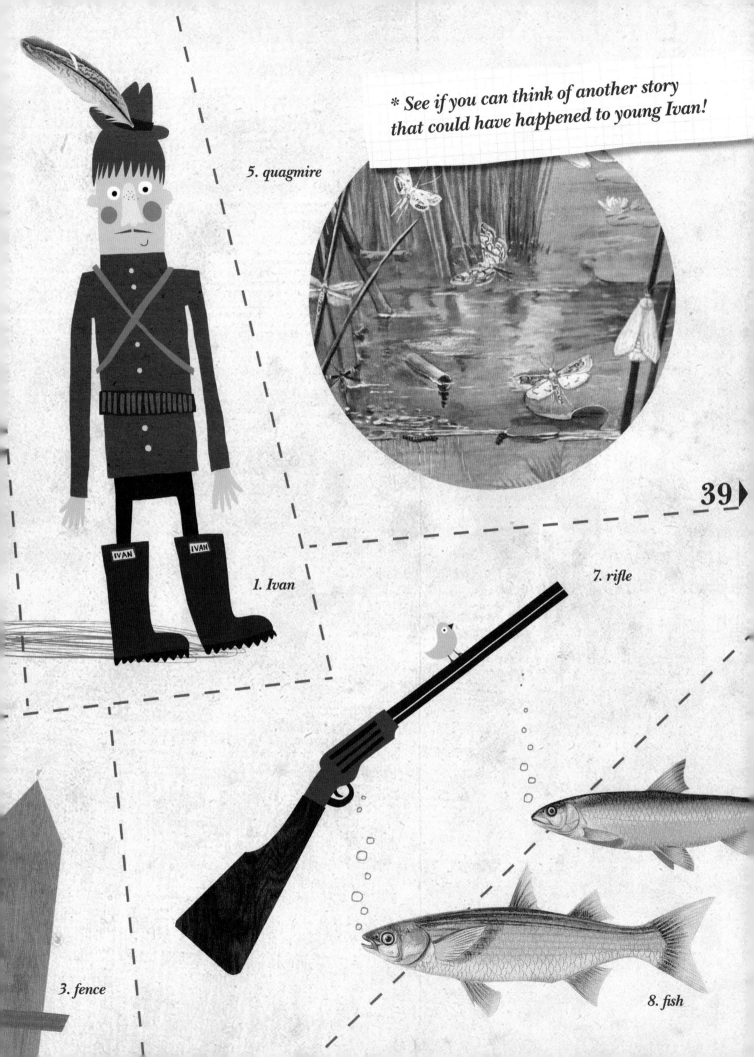

5. quagmire

* See if you can think of another story that could have happened to young Ivan!

39 ▶

1. Ivan

7. rifle

3. fence

8. fish

BALLOONS
Are Flying In The Sky...

Hold on!

Balloons are flying in the sky –
The sky is blue and bright.
Balloons are swishing in the sky
And glisten in their flight.

Balloons are flying on and on
While people wave to them.
Balloons are flying on and on,
And people wave to them.

Balloons are flying on and on,
And people wave their hats.
Balloons are flying on and on,
And people wave their sticks.

Balloons are flying on and on,
And people wave their buns.
Balloons are flying on and on,
And people wave their cats.

Balloons are flying on and on,
And people wave their stools.
Balloons are flying on and on,
And people wave their lamps.

Balloons are flying on and on,
And people gaze up high.
Balloons are glistening on and on
And swishing as they fly.
And the people, they watch and sigh.

1933

TIGER
IN THE STREET

I thought, long and hard, how the tiger made it into the street.
I was thinking, thinking, thinking,
I was guessing, guessing, guessing,
Then the wind came, strong and messy,
And I forgot what I was guessing.
So I never found out how the tiger made it into the street.

1936

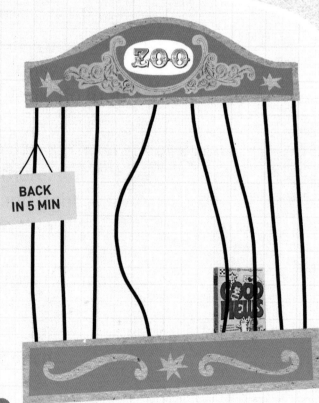

1. Run away from the zoo?

2. Came by ship from India?

Grandfather Tiger

3. Tiger's family always lived in this street!

THE MAN CAME OUT OF HIS HOME

A man came out of his home,
All set for far away.
He got his stick, he got his sack,
And soon was on his way.

He looked ahead, just straight ahead,
He walked and walked on foot.
No drink, no sleep,
No sleep, no drink,
No sleep, no drink, no food.

And then one day, at the crack of dawn
A forest rose there.
He entered it, and right away
He vanished into thin air.

So if you come across this man,
Or hear of him by chance.
Please waste no time, and let us know,
Please let us know at once.

1937

44

Acknowledgements

This book would never have appeared without the help and encouragement
of the people to whom I owe a huge debt of gratitude:

Mark Moncreiffe and Natalie Elsborg of Charles Russell LLP who were the first to provide encouragement to the idea of translating Kharms' work for children with their professional advice, their vivid and kind interest;

Elena Romaschenko who generously agreed that we could use her family photos of Leningrad in the 30s of the previous century – Kharms lived among those images and those people;

Natasha Vladimirskaya who proved to be my fortress and buttress;

Andrew Kostine who was my Virgil in the maze of the Russian copyright law;

Galina Dursthoff who made the arrangements with Kharms' heirs possible and provided immense support with her love of Russian literature;

The photograph of Daniil Kharms as a child was kindly provided by Galina from her extensive personal archive;

Katerina Akhtyrskaya whose brilliant skills were the key to fitting all our joint ideas into the book form;

Of course the brilliant, talented, spontaneous and breathtakingly creative illustrator Ksenia Kolosova whose vision of Kharms' images gave the book its present form;

And last but not least – my family who acted as financiers, multiple shoulders to cry on and endless listeners and commentators to concepts, translations, sources of knowledge and data, who made sure I always felt that Kharms' poetry was needed not only by Russian children but children of various countries and cultures who speak and read English.

Svetlana Dubovitskaya

Hopefully,
to be continued...

Bye!

for your
NOTES

Made in the USA
Lexington, KY
10 March 2014